S0-BBY-183

Q & A ABOUT

EARTH

NANCY DICKMANN

PowerKiDS
press

Published in 2018 by **The Rosen Publishing Group, Inc.**
29 East 21st Street, New York, NY 10010

Cataloging-in-Publication Data
Names: Dickmann, Nancy.
Title: Q & A about Earth / Nancy Dickmann.
Description: New York : PowerKids Press, 2018. | Series: Curious nature | Includes index.
Identifiers: ISBN 9781499433920 (pbk.) | ISBN 9781499433869 (library bound) | ISBN 9781499433746 (6 pack)
Subjects: LCSH: Earth (Planet)--Juvenile literature.
Classification: LCC QB631.4 D54 2018 | DDC 525--dc23

For Brown Bear Books Ltd:
Text and Editor: Nancy Dickmann
Editorial Director: Lindsey Lowe
Children's Publisher: Anne O'Daly
Design Manager: Keith Davis
Designer and Illustrator: Supriya Sahai
Picture Manager: Sophie Mortimer
Concept development: Square and Circus/Brown Bear Books Ltd

Picture Credits: All photographs copyright Shutterstock except Public Domain: Deep Sea News 23.

Brown Bear Books has made every attempt to contact the copyright holder.
If anyone has any information please contact licensing@brownbearbooks.co.uk

Manufactured in the United States of America

CPSIA Compliance Information: Batch BS17PK: For Further Information contact Rosen Publishing, New York, New York at 1-800-237-9932.

CONTENTS

WHAT IS A PLANET?

A planet is a large object in space. We live on a planet called Earth. It is an enormous ball of rock, thousands of miles wide. There are oceans, deserts, forests, and mountains on the surface.

Planets travel around a star. Earth moves around a star that we call the sun. Seven other planets travel around the sun. There are also smaller objects called asteroids. The sun, the planets, and other space objects make up our solar system.

GAS PLANETS

Not all planets are made of rock. Some planets are made of gas or ice. Jupiter is the biggest planet in the solar system. It is made of gas. Its stripes are bands of swirling clouds.

MANY MOONS

A moon is an object that travels around a planet. Our moon goes around Earth, not around the sun. Earth has one moon, but some planets have many more. Jupiter and Saturn have more than 60 each!

5

HOW FAR AWAY IS THE SUN?

The sun is about 93 million miles (150 million km) away from Earth. It is an enormous ball of glowing gas. Deep inside it, one kind of gas turns into another. This change releases energy. Some of it is light, and some is heat. The sun's energy travels to Earth. Without it, nothing could live on Earth.

The sun will keep shining for billions of years. Then it will run out of fuel. It will swell up, then fall in on itself.

AN ORDINARY STAR

The sun is the brightest object in the sky. It is a star, just like the other stars that twinkle in the night sky. The sun looks brighter than the other stars. That is because it is much closer to us.

TRAVELING TO THE SUN

Flying in a jet plane would take almost **19 years!**

Imagine if there was a road to the sun! How long would it take you to get there?

Walking would take you **3,539 years!**

Riding your bike would take **1,517 years.**

Plants need the sun's light to grow.

If you drove in a car, it would take **163 years.**

WHY CAN'T I DIG TO CHINA?

Have you ever dug a hole in your backyard? How deep did you go? You will never be able to dig all the way through the Earth. In fact, no one will!

In many places on Earth's surface, there is a layer of soil. It is several feet thick. If you dug far enough, you would hit solid rock. Underneath that is a very thick layer of hot rock. At the center of Earth is solid iron. No shovel can dig through that!

Land and the ocean floor are both part of Earth's crust

THE DEEPEST HOLE

The deepest hole ever dug is in Russia. Scientists dug 7.6 miles (12 km) into the ground. That still wasn't deep enough to reach Earth's mantle!

The **crust** is 3 to 30 miles (5 to 50 km) thick. It is made of solid rock and is thin but strong, like an eggshell. We live on the crust.

LAYERS OF THE EARTH

The **mantle** is 1,800 miles (2,900 km) thick. It is made of very hot rock. In some places the rock is so hot that it acts like a thick liquid.

The **outer core** is made of metal. It is so hot that the metal has melted into a liquid.

The **inner core** is a ball of solid metal. It is extremely hot.

9

CAN EARTH'S SURFACE MOVE?

Earth's crust is made of huge "plates" of rock. They fit together like a jigsaw puzzle. The plates float on top of the mantle. They move around, but very slowly. They move about as fast as your fingernails grow.

When two plates rub together, they can cause an earthquake. If it is a big earthquake, we can feel it on the surface. It feels like the ground is shaking.

Big earthquakes can make buildings collapse.

Most earthquakes happen in places where **two plates meet.**

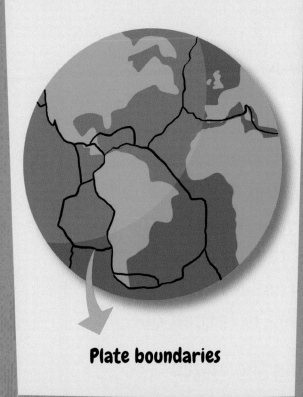

Plate boundaries

HOW EARTHQUAKES HAPPEN

1. Two plates **get stuck** as they try to slide past each other.

2. The longer they are stuck, the more **pressure** builds up.

3. The plates finally move. The stored-up pressure makes them move a long way in a short time. This is an **earthquake.**

MEASURING EARTHQUAKES

Scientists use tools to measure how much the Earth moves. They figure out how much energy is released. They give this a number, such as 6. The higher the number, the more powerful the quake.

11

WHY DO VOLCANOES ERUPT?

A volcano is a place where melted rock comes up from underground. The melted rock is called magma. Magma is lighter than solid rock. It rises toward the surface. When it rises, it creates pressure. When a volcano erupts, the magma is forced out.

Volcanoes often form along the edges of Earth's plates. Many volcanoes are cracks in the Earth's surface. Other volcanoes are mountains.

Magma is called lava once it erupts onto the surface.

WHAT COMES OUT OF A VOLCANO?

Clouds of **ash** come out of a volcano. The ash can fall like snow.

Some volcanoes shoot out **solid rocks**.

Hot **gases** come out when a volcano erupts. Water vapor is the most common gas. Deadly gases are released, too.

MUD VOLCANOES

Some volcanoes shoot out mud. They don't produce lava, so they are not true volcanoes. The mud forms when hot water from deep underground mixes with dirt or other materials.

Sometimes **melted rock** comes out of a volcano. It can shoot up into the sky, or ooze down the side. When it cools, it gets hard.

13

WHERE DO FOSSILS COME FROM?

Fossils are the remains of plants and animals that died long ago. Most of the soft body parts rot away. The hard parts can get preserved in rock as fossils. Scientists have found fossils of dinosaur bones. There are fossils of seashells, plants, and even eggs.

Most fossils form underground. Scientists dig these fossils out of the ground. Fossils show us what animals and plants were like long ago.

Fossils of footprints can show us how dinosaurs walked.

NOT JUST BONES

Many fossils are body parts, but some are not. Scientists have found fossils of dinosaur footprints. There are even fossils of dinosaur poop!

HOW SOME FOSSILS FORM

A dinosaur dies.

The dead body is washed into a lake or river.

The dinosaur's flesh rots away. Hard bones are left behind. The skeleton gets buried in mud.

Over millions of years, more mud piles up. Minerals in the water seep into the bones.

The layers of mud harden into rock. The bones harden too. They are now fossils.

WHERE DOES THE SUN GO AT NIGHT?

When the sun sets, it seems to disappear. But it is just on the other side of Earth, where you can't see it. When the sun goes down, it is night on your side of the planet. For someone standing on the other side of Earth, it is daytime. They can see the sun in the sky.

The Earth spins around and around. It makes a complete circle once every 24 hours. This movement makes the sun seem to travel across the sky.

When the sun goes down, the sky changes color.

DAYTIME MOON

We only see the sun during the day. But the moon can appear at night or in the day! The moon travels around the Earth. From where you are, you can see it about half the time. It is very bright at night, but less bright during the day.

DAY AND NIGHT

The sun sends out light and heat in all directions.

You

Sometimes the part of Earth that you are on is facing the sun. It is daytime for you. On the other side of the planet, it is night.

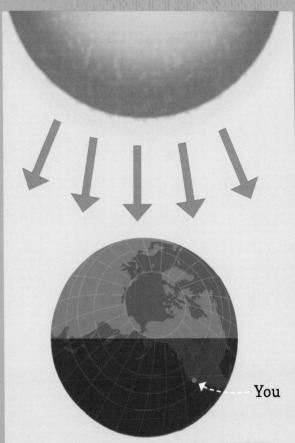

You

When your part of the Earth faces away from the sun, it is night for you.

WHAT IS AIR MADE OF?

You cannot see air. You cannot feel it, either. But the air around us is made up of tiny particles of gas. The gas particles are much too small to see or feel.

Air is a mixture of different gases. The main one is nitrogen. There is oxygen, too. Animals need oxygen to breathe. Air also has water vapor. This is water in the form of a gas.

AIR POLLUTION
Sometimes other substances get into the air. This is called pollution. Dust, germs, and harmful gases can cause air pollution. Breathing polluted air can cause health problems.

Most weather is in the lower levels of the atmosphere.

THE ATMOSPHERE
The air that surrounds Earth is called the atmosphere.

The atmosphere is about 300 miles (480 km) thick. At the top, the air is too thin to breathe.

The **atmosphere** has different layers.

The weight of the air presses down on us. This is called **air pressure**.

Plants need air. They take in carbon dioxide gas from the air. They give out oxygen.

WHY DOES THE SEA GO IN AND OUT?

Sometimes the sea is a long way out, making a beach look big. At other times the water comes farther in, covering the sand. These changes happen because of tides.

Tides are made by the moon. Every object in space pulls on objects around it. The bigger an object is, the stronger its pull. This pull is called gravity. The moon's gravity affects the ocean. This causes tides.

TIDE POOLS

Many beaches have tide pools. These rocky areas are covered with water during high tide. At low tide, they are exposed. Plants and animals must be able to survive these different conditions.

Starfish often live in tide pools.

HOW THE MOON MAKES TIDES

Between the two bulges, the water is lower. This is **low tide**.

The moon's gravity pulls on the Earth. It makes the ocean's waters bulge. This part of the Earth has a **high tide**.

The moon travels around the Earth. At the same time, the Earth spins. This makes the areas of high tide move.

On the opposite side, there is another **high tide bulge**.

HOW DEEP IS THE OCEAN?

Near the coast, the ocean is shallow. Farther out, it gets deeper. The deepest point is in the Mariana Trench. It is nearly 36,000 feet (11,000 m) deep. That's deeper than Mount Everest is tall.

The deeper you go in the ocean, the darker it gets. The water gets colder, too. The huge weight of the water above presses down.

Deep **trenches** cut through the ocean floor in some places.

THE OCEAN FLOOR

Most of the ocean floor is **flat** and deep.

DEEP-SEA EXPLORERS

Scientists have been to the deepest part of the ocean. They travel in special vehicles. These vehicles are very strong. They protect their passengers from the crushing pressure.

This vehicle is called Alvin. It can dive to 14,764 feet (4,500 m).

Sometimes volcanoes grow so tall that they reach the surface. They are now **islands.**

At the edge of a land mass, the ocean is **shallow.**

There are many cone-shaped **volcanoes** under the sea.

Farther out, the ocean floor **slopes** steeply down.

WHERE DO RIVERS GO?

Many rivers start as small streams, high in the mountains. They flow downhill and join up with other streams. Rain and melting snow add more water. Eventually it becomes a large river. The river keeps flowing until it empties into the sea. Rivers are an important part of the water cycle.

CANYONS

As rivers flow, they wear away the ground around them. Over many years, they can carve deep grooves in the rock. These are called canyons. Some canyons are thousands of feet deep.

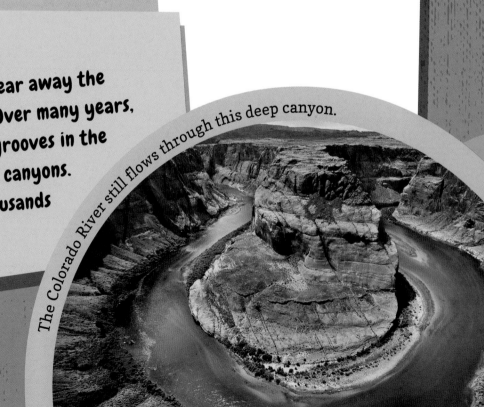

The Colorado River still flows through this deep canyon.

THE WATER CYCLE

The **sun** heats the Earth's surface.

High in the sky, the water vapor forms **clouds**.

Water in oceans, rivers, and lakes warms up. It evaporates and rises into the air as **water vapor**.

Water falls from the clouds as **rain**. It falls on the oceans and the land.

On land, some of the water flows into **rivers**. The rivers take it to the ocean. The cycle begins again.

WHO LIVES ON PLANET EARTH?

We do! There are more than 7 billion people on Earth. People live in villages, towns, and cities. Some live in warm places, and some in cold places.

We share our planet with other living things. Plants and animals live in almost every corner of the Earth. They live in many different biomes. A biome is a large area with similar weather and land.

LIFE ON OTHER PLANETS?

So far, Earth is the only place we know that has life. However, there may be life on other planets or moons. One day we may discover it!

More than half of the Earth's people live in busy cities.

26

THE WORLD'S BIOMES

Deserts are very dry. They are usually hot too. Plants and animals here must find and store water.

Trees grow thick and tall in a **forest**. Many animals live in their branches.

Fish, whales, and many other creatures live in **water**.

It is cold and snowy in the **polar regions**. Animals here have thick fur to keep them warm.

Grasslands have grass, but few trees. Animals graze on their grasses.

Mountain slopes can be barren and rocky. Trees grow on the lower slopes.

27

MAKE A SUNDIAL

The sun makes shadows on the ground. As the sun moves across the sky, the shadows move, too. You can use these shadows to tell the time. All you need is a sundial.

WHAT YOU NEED

* paper plate
* plastic straw
* sharpened pencil
* pen or marker
* ruler
* clock or watch

1 Use the pencil to poke a hole in the center of the plate. Write a "12" on the edge of the plate. Use the ruler to draw a line from the number to the center.

2 Stick the straw into the hole. Tilt it slightly toward your line.

3 Wait for a dry, sunny day. Take your sundial outside at noon. Turn it until the straw's shadow points to the 12.

5 At 1:00 p.m., make a mark where the shadow falls. Label it "1."

4 Make sure that the plate can't move around. (You could use some stones or other weights to hold it in place.)

6 Every hour, mark the new time. Continue the next morning until you get back to noon.

TELLING THE TIME
Over the next few weeks, check your sundial against a clock. How accurate is it?

GLOSSARY

atmosphere layers of gases that surround the Earth

core very center of something

crust thin outer layer of the Earth, made of hard rock

energy ability to do work

erupt break or burst out suddenly

evaporate turn from a liquid into a gas

fossil remains of a living thing from a long time ago that are trapped in rock

gas form of matter that is not solid or liquid

gravity force that pulls objects toward each other; on Earth, gravity pulls everything down toward the ground

magma hot, melted rock underground

mantle layer of the Earth between the crust and the core

mineral nonliving substance that is formed in the earth

moon large natural object that travels around a planet

oxygen gas in the air that living things need

particle very tiny piece of something

plate boundaries places where the plates of Earth's crust meet

preserved kept in its original state

pressure force of something pushing

star huge ball of glowing gas in space

tides rising and falling of sea levels caused by the moon

volcano opening in Earth's crust that lets out gases and melted rock

water vapor water that is in the form of gas

FURTHER RESOURCES

BOOKS

Claybourne, Anna. *Encyclopedia of Planet Earth.* Tulsa, OK: Usborne Books, 2013.

Taylor-Butler, Christine. *Planet Earth.* New True Books: Space. Danbury, CT: Children's Press, 2014.

Tomecek, Steve. *Dirtmeister's Nitty Gritty Planet Earth: All About Rocks, Minerals, Fossils, Earthquakes, Volcanoes, & Even Dirt!* National Geographic Kids. Washington, DC: National Geographic Children's Books, 2015.

Van Rose, Susanna. *Earth.* DK Eyewitness Books. New York: Dorling Kindersley, 2013.

Walpole, Brenda. *I Wonder Why The Sun Rises: and Other Questions About Time and Seasons.* I Wonder Why. New York: Kingfisher Books, 2011.

WEBSITES

Due to the changing nature of Internet links, PowerKids Press has developed an online list of websites related to the subject of this book. This site is updated regularly.

Please use this link to access the list:
www.powerkidslinks.com/cn/earth

INDEX